Do You Want To Play With My Balls?

by The Cifaldi Brothers
illustrated by Santiago Elizalde

ISBN 978-0-9859487-1-9
First edition 2012
Fourth Printing 2015

Printed in the United States of America

Copyright © 2012 Bum Bum Books, LLC
Ann Arbor, MI USA
www.bumbumbooks.com

The first ever Bum Bum Book!

Hey Louie! Do you want to play with my balls?

Sure Chuck! I can hold your ball sack so it won't drag on the ground.

Wow! Your balls are so big, I can't even fit them in my mouth!

My mom's always yelling, 'Louie! Get those balls out of your mouth before you choke!'

You know that mean girl Sally?

She squeezed my balls so hard they looked funny.

Yeah, well when I play
with Sally …

I always end up with blue balls.

Billy Johnson made Sally cry last week. Now that kid's got balls!

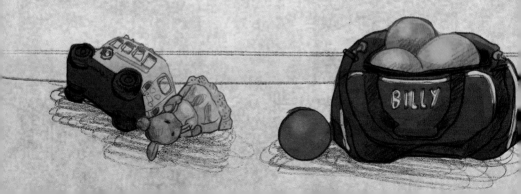

Not anymore ... yesterday
Sally kicked Billy's balls so
hard he lost one.

Look Louie!

Your dog is licking my balls!

Let's roll them on Sparky's fur. Girls hate hairy balls!

You know Chuck, if we show Sally our hairy balls, she'll scream for sure!

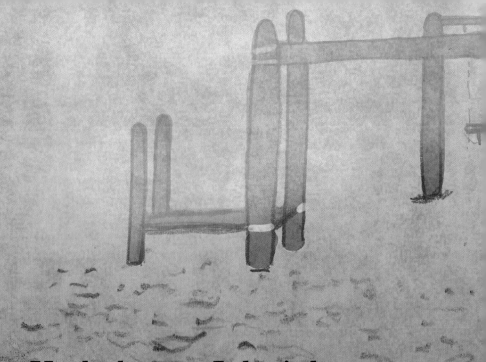

Yeah, but ... I don't know.
I kind of like Sally. I wish
she would just play nice
with my balls.

Yeah, me too.

Hi Sally! Do you want to play with our balls?

Sure! But only if I can play with both of your balls at the same time!

The End